1X $^{11}/_{12}$ Lt $^{12}/_{10}$

in the news™

LIVING GREEN

Jeanne Nagle

ROSEN
PUBLISHING®

New York

To Ray, who someday may use science
to protect the environment and help people

Published in 2009 by The Rosen Publishing Group, Inc.
29 East 21st Street, New York, NY 10010

First Edition

Library of Congress Cataloging-in-Publication Data

Nagle, Jeanne M.
Living green / Jeanne Nagle.
    p. cm.—(In the news)
Includes bibliographical references and index.
ISBN-13: 978-1-4358-5037-8 (library binding)
ISBN-13: 978-1-4358-5365-2 (pbk)
ISBN-13: 978-1-4358-5371-3 (6 pack)
1. Environmental responsibility. 2. Green movement. 3. Sustainable living. I. Title.
GE195.7.N34 2009
333.72—dc22

                                                      2008013560

Manufactured in Malaysia

On the cover: Clockwise from top left: Green construction extends all the way to a building's rooftop garden; eco-friendly cars are main attractions at car shows these days; international government panels hash out rules, guidelines, and goals designed to boost green living efforts.

contents

Why Living Green Matters

Green has become a very hot color, and not just for its pleasant aesthetic qualities. It is the shade most commonly seen in and associated with nature (grass, plants, and trees). As such, green has achieved an elevated status in countries around the globe as the symbol of environmentally friendly products, practices, and lifestyle choices. People who make a conscious effort to protect the environment are thus said to be "living green."

Living green involves seeking a balance that lets humans exist in harmony with nature, other living creatures, and each other, while still enjoying a decent quality of life. Humans work to become good enough stewards, or caretakers, of the planet so that "Mother Earth" may continue to provide the things people need to survive, like oxygen, shelter, healthy food, and clean water. Green living also seeks to prevent or repair damage done to the planet through the actions of humankind. For instance, pollution ruins the air, the soil

People everywhere, like these New Zealanders, are hearing and answering the environment's distress call.

in which crops grow, and bodies of water. Part of living green, then, involves finding ways to reduce or eliminate pollution.

Green Is Everywhere

There is practically no area of human activity that cannot be performed in a more environmentally friendly manner. Reporter Scott Streater surveyed professors, scientists, and energy experts to discover the most important

Produce that's grown locally and free of pesticides is an excellent green food choice.

aspects of a green life. They are, as outlined in Streater's article:

- Travel: Finding ways to get from place to place that don't involve the burning of fossil fuels (oil and gasoline) and the emitting of toxic fumes, as cars, buses, and planes do.
- Water: Saving water supplies from overuse and pollution.
- Food: Choosing items that are grown both locally (to avoid emissions from transportation) and organically (meaning not sprayed with dangerous chemicals).
- Energy efficiency: Using cleaner, renewable energy resources.
- Recycling: Using materials more than once reduces gas emissions from landfills (dumps) and means that less energy is used to create new items.

Pick up any newspaper or magazine, surf the Internet, or watch your favorite talk shows on television, and you're bound to come across stories about living a green life. It seems as if the world is in the midst of a green revolution. Why this should be the case makes sense when you consider a few key factors that influence the decision to live green: the effect of climate change, the influence of the media, and our increasingly inter-dependent world.

The Issue of Climate Change

Scientists have studied Earth's climate, or weather patterns, for hundreds of years. It wasn't until 1896, however, that a Swedish chemist named Svante Arrhenius first proposed the idea that human activity could greatly affect the environment. While trying to explain what happened to bring about the end of the Ice Age millions of years before, Arrhenius discovered what has become known as the greenhouse effect. This is the concept that atmospheric gases such as carbon dioxide let sunlight through to warm the planet, but then trap enough heat radiating back from Earth's surface to sustain life on the planet. If too much gas gathers in the atmosphere, however, too much of the sun's heat becomes trapped, causing temperatures to rise unnaturally and the climate to change.

Later in life, Arrhenius would receive the Nobel Prize in Chemistry for other scientific discoveries. At the

Svante Arrhenius is credited with discovering the cause of climate change.

time, though, his research on the greenhouse effect was questioned by the scientific community and ignored by the general public. Yet, climate studies in the 1970s began to show that Arrhenius might be on to something. They concluded that not only was his theory a reality, but also that the level of certain gases connected to the greenhouse effect were on the rise. Rising temperatures change Earth's climate enough to create all sorts of weather-related problems, including hurricanes, floods, and wildfires. Scientists also determined that human activity was resulting in a dramatic increase of those gas levels in the atmosphere, which was a major cause of a developing climate change.

Once North America started to experience record-setting high temperatures in the summer—beginning in 1988 and continuing to this day—people began to think that the notion of climate change should be taken seriously as a threat not only to the environment but also to life on Earth. They wanted governments and industry to stop polluting, which helps cause greenhouse gas buildup in the atmosphere. On an individual level, people began taking steps that would help reduce their personal contribution to greenhouse gas emissions. This is when interest in the green living movement really began to gather steam.

Science Points the Way

How do we know for sure that climate change exists or that human-made greenhouse gases are the cause of rising temperatures? We must rely on scientific evidence. A lot has changed since Arrhenius's day. Modern researchers have had the benefit of using sophisticated tools and methods such as satellites and computer-generated mathematical models. Modeling involves using data and mathematical formulas to prove theories, illustrate concepts, and explain processes. Climate models allow scientists to more accurately determine past and future weather patterns. These models also help researchers determine what might be causing changes in Earth's climate.

Research has shown what part people have played in the buildup of greenhouse gases. In 1981, James Hansen and Andrew Lacis, scientists at the National Aeronautics and Space Administration's Goddard

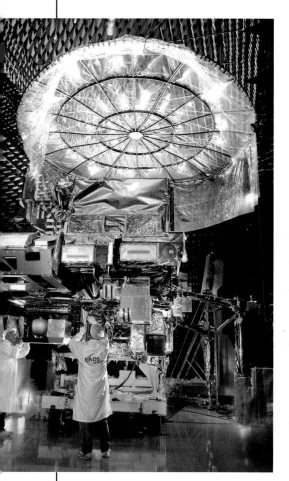

Satellites like Europe's MetOp-A make weather research much easier, more accurate, and more comprehensive.

Institute for Space Studies, designed a model that would show how atmospheric changes affected average temperatures on Earth. They added information about gases and chemicals created by humans and commonly released into the atmosphere so that the model would imitate weather conditions as if they were influenced by the greenhouse effect. The research proved that human-produced gases, especially carbon dioxide, do have a warming effect on the world's climate.

Since then, many other climate change studies have been conducted by universities, government- and privately owned research centers, and respected science organizations such as the National Academy of Sciences and the American Association for the Advancement of Science. The consensus, or general agreement, created by their findings is that there is a connection between human activity and global warming.

This conclusion has been approved and confirmed by the Intergovernmental Panel on Climate Change, the Nobel Prize–winning organization created by the United Nations to evaluate climate science research and reports. Humankind's ties to climate change also have the backing of respected organizations that are quite knowledgeable regarding climate and weather issues, including the American Meteorological Society and the American Geophysical Union.

Media Coverage

Of course, all the scientific proof in the world cannot convince people to adopt a green lifestyle if the information is not made readily available to them. In the past, a lot of studies on climate change have circulated within the scientific community only, published in journals that the general public would not have known existed or could not easily obtain.

Average citizens in the United States report that they get most of their information from the mainstream media—television, radio, newspapers, magazines, and the Internet. The American news media has been covering climate change, on and off, since 1950, yet few people paid attention at first or felt compelled to act. At the time, the idea of global warming and the destruction it could cause seemed pretty abstract. It

Why Earth is heating up

How burning fossil fuels and other human activity are contributing to a warmer planet:

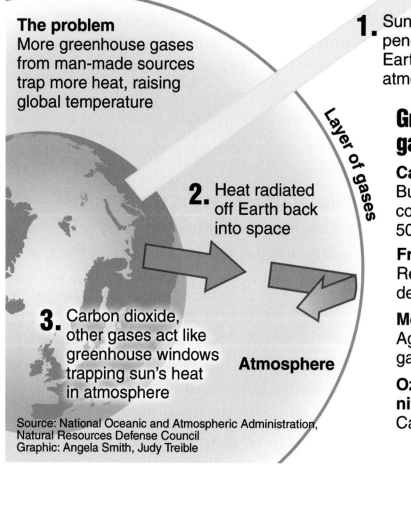

The problem
More greenhouse gases from man-made sources trap more heat, raising global temperature

1. Sun's rays penetrate Earth's atmosphere

Layer of gases

2. Heat radiated off Earth back into space

3. Carbon dioxide, other gases act like greenhouse windows trapping sun's heat in atmosphere

Atmosphere

Greenhouse gases

Carbon dioxide
Burning oil, gas, coal; more than 50% of the gases

Freon
Refrigerant, detergent

Methane
Agriculture, oil, gas pipelines

Ozone, nitrous oxide
Car exhaust

Source: National Oceanic and Atmospheric Administration, Natural Resources Defense Council
Graphic: Angela Smith, Judy Treible

© 2006 MCT

The Internet is a prime source for information on climate change and living green.

was difficult to understand and didn't seem to offer much concrete proof.

All that changed a few decades later. When information concerning the connection between climate change and natural disasters started appearing alongside stories about the latest Category 5 hurricane or devastating flood, people began to take notice at last. Finally, they could vividly see and understand the very real threat posed by climate change, and many people decided to change their lifestyles in the hope of easing the problem. Media coverage of the deadly European heat wave in 2003 and the intense North American hurricane seasons of 2004 and 2005 (including the devastation wrought by Hurricane Katrina in New Orleans and throughout the Gulf states) are recent examples of news stories that have convinced people to start living green.

The Importance of Interdependence

In nature, communities called ecosystems exist because of a concept known as interdependence. This is when all living things in a particular environment help each other survive. Each plant and creature takes what it needs from the community, like food and shelter, and in return provides for other members of the ecosystem as well.

Interdependence is like a chain. When something happens to disturb or break just one link, the entire chain becomes weaker. In 2007, the world witnessed an example of this concept in action when huge numbers of honeybees mysteriously disappeared across North America. Bees pollinate, or fertilize, the flowers that bloom on crops so that they will grow into fruits and vegetables. In return, the flowers provide nectar, which is bee food. Without enough bees to pollinate fields, farmers had a difficult time growing several types of crops. Without honeybees, fewer fruits and vegetables were available in the supermarket, and prices for those that were available increased.

The relationship between humans and nature is also interdependent. Earth provides food, medicine, building materials, and so much more to humans. If the relationship is truly interdependent, then humans should take care of and protect Earth as well, for their own sake if not for nobler reasons. Our own survival depends on maintaining a healthy planet. The growing number of people who feel this way show they care by trying to live green.

Another interdependent relationship that encourages green living exists among people from different lands, within the large ecosystem that is our planet. Dramatic advances in communications technology and transportation have meant greater connections among the nations of the world, especially when it comes to business. Consequently, the understanding that the actions of one country impact the global community as a whole is clearer than ever before.

Boundaries that used to separate us—social, economic, and even environmental—are now being crossed all the time. As detailed in a *Science Daily* article in 2003, mercury from forest fires in Canada's old-growth forests drifted into the northeastern United States,

Humans depend on natural resources, such as the honeybee, to keep food on their plates.

where it polluted the air and may eventually settle in lakes and streams, poisoning the fish that live there.

The chance that our actions could negatively affect nations with whom we do business—and whom we, therefore, cannot afford to alienate—drives many corporations and their shareholders to consider switching to green business practices. On a more personal level, it convinces individuals to go green out of respect for their international neighbors and in the name of cooperation and brotherhood.

Green Pioneers, Then and Now

2

D
espite its recent popularity, green living is not a new phenomenon. The principles behind living green have been around and put into practice for quite a while. For instance, when their forests were being stripped of trees to provide heating fuel, the citizens of ancient Greece began to position their buildings to make the most of solar heat instead.

In the Middle East, between the eighth and thirteenth centuries, scientists and philosophers wrote medical documents concerning air, water, and soil pollution, as well as how to properly dispose of solid waste (human waste and trash). Environmental impact assessments, which determine the likely effect that building and farming will have on the environment, were also conducted in Muslim countries around this time.

The situation was similar in medieval England. In 1306, King Edward I made it illegal to burn coal in London. He was trying to improve the air quality of the city, which had a perpetual smog hanging over it due to coal fires.

Founding Environmentalists

Efforts to live in an environmentally friendly manner took place in the United States even before the nation's official birth in 1776. One of the country's founding fathers, Ben Franklin (1706–1790), fought long and hard for clean water in Philadelphia. In 1739, he was part of a group that tried to get the state of Pennsylvania to outlaw industrial waste dumping that was believed to be polluting the city's water supply. Franklin even left instructions in his will that his money be used to construct a pipeline that would deliver fresh water to the city.

Another signer of the Declaration of Independence, Thomas Jefferson (1743–1826), was also among the earliest environmentalists in the United States. He practiced a green lifestyle on his farm in Virginia. Aware that farming, cutting down trees for lumber, and other human interference with nature took a toll on the land, Jefferson made a point of conserving the natural resources in his possession. He rotated his crops to different locations after a few seasons and fertilized using manure, which was not a common practice at the time. Both practices returned important nutrients back into the depleted soil.

Plowing horizontally over slopes, not cutting down too many trees, and planting different kinds of grass for

From his hilltop Virginia home, Monticello, Thomas Jefferson could keep watch over the surrounding farmland.

ground cover were methods Jefferson used to prevent the top layer of soil from eroding. Because he supported agricultural education, he freely shared these and other techniques with other farmers. Some historians also think his environmental beliefs spilled over into policies he enacted while president. As author Peter Ling wrote in the January 2004 issue of *History Today*, President Jefferson favored agrarian (land and agriculture) initiatives over those that centered on industrial development.

The Poet and the Preservationist

Two men in nineteenth-century America have each been labeled "the father of environmentalism." The first is Henry David Thoreau (1817–1862), an author, poet, teacher, and philosopher who studied and deeply appreciated nature. Thoreau believed humans should conserve Earth's natural resources such as trees and soil. He also spoke out about preserving forests and other natural areas, which means keeping them in as natural and unspoiled a state as possible.

Thoreau took living green to the extreme when he spent two years living in the woods near Concord, Massachusetts. He built himself a cabin on Walden Pond and spent time tending a garden, writing, and observing nature. This was a way for him to live simply, relying on nature and his own industry to provide him with food, shelter, clothing, and fuel. In return, he would protect the nature that sustained and nurtured him. The experience was the inspiration for his book *Walden* (1854), which is considered one of the greatest books ever written on nature and living green.

The other man who is considered "the father of environmentalism" is John Muir (1838–1914). A Scottish immigrant to America, Muir held a number of jobs in his lifetime, including rancher, shepherd, sawmill manager, ferry operator, and bronco buster. But what he preferred

The friendship between John Muir *(right)* and Theodore Roosevelt resulted in greater protection of natural areas in the United States, including the creation of national parks.

to do was study nature. An amateur scientist and geologist, he spent as much time as he could climbing mountains and examining glaciers. Like Thoreau, Muir built himself a cabin near the water, in California's Yosemite Valley, a place he called "the grandest of all special temples of Nature."

Best known as the founder and first president of the Sierra Club—begun in 1892 and still one of the most respected environmental organizations in the United States—Muir wanted to preserve wilderness areas. To accomplish this, he envisioned setting up a large system of national parks such as Yellowstone, which had come under protection of the federal government in 1872.

Muir wrote several influential essays and books on the subject that caught the attention of congressmen and other officials in Washington, D.C. Owing in part to these writings, Congress created Yosemite National Park in 1890. Muir's beloved Yosemite Valley, however, was not included in the deal. That area wouldn't be made part of the park until 1905, under President Theodore Roosevelt.

A Conservationist in the White House

An active naturalist even before he became president in 1901, Theodore "Teddy" Roosevelt (1858–1919) was able to put his conservation beliefs into action while he was in office. He passed many laws and acts that protected thousands of acres of wilderness.

In addition to the expansion at Yosemite, Roosevelt was responsible for the creation of five additional national parks. He also signed the Antiquities Act, a law that allowed him to establish eighteen national monuments. A national monument is a natural structure that exists on U.S.-owned property and, like a national park, enjoys the protection of the federal government.

Saving the environment in this manner wasn't easy. Congress did not always agree with Roosevelt's policies. Congress wanted unlimited access to the wilderness so that America could profit from its natural resources, especially timber and coal. To protect the forests, Roosevelt expanded the role of the Bureau of Forestry (today the National Forest Service) to include conservation and "wise use" management of federally owned woods.

Women Take the Lead

In the 1920s and 1930s, increased industrialization began taking a noticeable toll on the environment through pollution and a depletion of some natural resources. Humans, too, began to suffer as a result of environmental degradation. The green living focus then switched from preserving the wilderness to protecting both environmental and human health and well-being. At the head of this new fight was Alice Hamilton (1869–1970), a doctor, researcher, and educator who brought attention to the link between human-made environmental toxins and serious illnesses.

Hamilton investigated health risks that occurred on the job, first for the city of Chicago, then as an unpaid employee of the federal government. She scientifically documented the harmful effects of toxic, or poisonous, substances commonly created by the materials and processes used in workplaces of the time. These included carbon monoxide in the steel industry; mercury in hat making; and, most notably, lead in the enamel, automotive, and petroleum industries.

Many of the toxic dangers Hamilton researched remain a threat to humans and the environment today. As documented in several news reports, lead poisoning from toys made in China became a huge issue in 2007. Trace amounts of lead can also be found in incandescent light bulbs, which is what most people still use instead of newer energy-saving compact florescent bulbs. And carbon monoxide, generated by automobiles, is considered a greenhouse gas. Hamilton paved the way for a greater understanding of hazardous chemicals that are threats to a safe, green life, but we have only just begun to act upon her warnings.

Dr. Alice Hamilton fought to keep environmental threats from harming people.

In the 1960s, another woman raised awareness of the damage done by one specific environmental toxin. Rachel Carson (1907–1964) was a marine biologist with the U.S. Fish and Wildlife Service before she became a respected nature author. Her first three books, one of which was a *New York Times* best seller, discussed the interdependence of life in the sea. Then she turned her attention to DDT, a powerful and deadly pesticide that was used on farms and orchards to get rid of insects.

DDT killed just about every bug in its path. The problem was that not all insects harmed crops. In fact, some, like bees, were needed for pollination. On top of

Banning poisonous chemicals sprayed on crops was biologist Rachel Carson's greatest goal.

that, birds were also dying because of the pesticide. In her book *Silent Spring*, published in 1962, Carson detailed all of this, as well as how DDT stayed strong for a long time and didn't wash away in the rain. She showed how DDT could enter the human food chain and give people cancer.

Eventually, because of Carson's pioneering research and passionate arguments, DDT was banned. Another important result was a renewed interest in environmentalism. Carson had gotten the attention of millions of people with *Silent Spring*. Readers agreed with her green philosophy, which she shared during a 1964 interview: "Man's attitude toward nature is today critically important simply because we have now acquired a fateful power to alter and destroy nature. But man is a part of nature, and his war against nature is inevitably a war against himself."

Paying Dearly for the Cause

Ken Saro-Wiwa (1941–1995) didn't have to get involved in the conflict between his Ogoni people and those who controlled Nairobi's oil interests in the African nation of Kenya. A former government employee, Saro-Wiwa was also a successful journalist, author, and television producer. He was not like the Ogoni farmers whose land and livelihoods had been ruined by extensive oil drilling. And yet he did get involved, writing books about the Ogoni situation and being arrested several times for his actions.

Saro-Wiwa also helped organize the activist group Movement for the Survival of the Ogoni People, which demanded payment for privately owned land devastated by drilling and a fair portion of oil profits. In 1993, the group staged a massive march to protest the uncontrolled oil spills and acid rain that ruined the region's soil and water, killing fish and wildlife in the area.

Many consider Ken Saro-Wiwa, seen on this poster, to be a national hero in Kenya for his attempts to protect the Ogoni people and their ancestral lands from big oil interests.

The protest was peaceful, but the government's response was not. Hundreds of Ogoni were thrown in jail, and their villages were looted and burned. Saro-Wiwa was arrested, tried, and convicted for murders he did not commit and was later hanged. As widely reported by friends and family members, Saro-Wiwa, aware of his impending fate, said from jail, "I'll tell you this. I may be dead, but my ideas will not die."

America's Latest Environmental Crusader

Former U.S. vice president Al Gore (b. 1948) has a new job these days—international spokesperson for the environment. Gore earned that title after the success of the 2006 movie *An Inconvenient Truth* and his best-selling book of the same name. The film and book document the threat of global warming, as well as what people can do to help the planet avoid an ecological meltdown.

Gore has had a longstanding respect for nature, and his interest in global warming dates back to his time in college. As a U.S. senator in the early 1990s, he was responsible for congressional hearings on the subject. As vice president of the United States, he sought environmental reforms, including a tax on fossil fuel use called a carbon tax. He also helped put together 1997's Kyoto Protocol, an international agreement to reduce greenhouse gas emissions (discussed in Chapter 3).

Al Gore has gone on the road to talk about concepts examined in the movie *An Inconvenient Truth.*

Though he no longer holds political office, Gore is still an environmental activist. In 2004, he started Generation Investment Management, a firm that helps clients invest money in pro-green companies that have shown they take the interdependence between humans and nature seriously. Along with the United Nations' Intergovernmental Panel on Climate Change, Gore was the 2007 Nobel Peace Prize winner. The award was given in recognition of his work on climate change.

The Green Machine: Politics, Law, and Power

Choosing to adopt a green lifestyle is a very personal decision. Each individual has to figure out what he or she can do, and how far to take it. For example, maybe someone thinks riding a bike to work would be too impractical or difficult but doesn't mind taking a little extra time to locate and buy locally grown, organic produce or recycled paper products.

So, on a personal level, people decide for themselves whether or not they want to live green and to what extent. However, on a nationwide level, individuals are not the only ones involved in the decision-making process. Governments also have influence over how green our lives can and should be.

Legislating the Environment

The way that governments control human interaction with the environment is to legislate, which means to pass laws. Traditionally, environmental laws have sought to preserve the wilderness (as when Theodore Roosevelt created national parks and monuments), conserve a country's natural resources, or reduce pollution.

Most of the world's developed countries have passed environmental laws. A developed country is a nation that has plenty of industry, advanced technology, and a relatively high standard of living. Several nations, including South Africa, South Korea, China, and virtually every nation in the European Union, have the right to a clean, safe environment written directly into their constitutions. Whether or not this right is actually honored by the nations' governments is a matter of debate. Still, these countries have made living green a constitutional right for their citizens, much like U.S. citizens have freedom of speech, thought, religion, and other freedoms spelled out in the Bill of Rights.

The Environmental Protection Agency

To make sure that America's ecological laws are followed, the country has the Environmental Protection Agency (EPA), a department of the federal government designed to protect America's natural environment. Before the EPA was established in 1970, the government had to rely on several small departments with various specialty areas

The EPA has been fighting air pollution from motor vehicles for decades.

to fight pollution and other environmental problems. Bringing all those departments into one agency gave the United States more coordinated and effective green power.

The main jobs of the EPA are setting standards and regulating environmentally safe behavior, as well as enforcing environmental laws at the state and national level. One of the first and largest pieces of legislation over which the EPA gained control is the Clean Air Act of 1970. The Clean Air Act combats air pollution by developing regulations to control toxic emissions from moving vehicles and industrial sources. Major amendments, or added improvements, that sought to make the air even safer and cleaner were made to the act in 1977 and 1990.

The EPA has the power to punish people and organizations that break environmental laws by charging fines or limiting a company's ability to conduct business within the United States, generally referred to as a sanction. The EPA also conducts research and oversees many pollution prevention and energy conservation programs of its own.

The Politics of Climate Change

Greenhouse gases and global warming have raised awareness of the need for green living. Naturally, they have also become an important focus of environmental policy and legislation as well.

In America, it is primarily state and local governments that are responsible for laws on climate change, like California's regulations targeting the reduction of carbon dioxide emissions from automobile exhaust. As of early 2008, there were no federal laws concerning greenhouse gas emissions, but not from a lack of trying. Throughout the years, a number of bills aimed at combating global warming have been presented to Congress, but none of them have been passed into law. For example, in 2004, Senators John McCain and Joseph Lieberman introduced the Climate Stewardship Act. The bill gave industry six years to reduce emissions of greenhouse gases, including carbon dioxide, to pre-2001 levels. The bill failed by a 53–44 vote.

Another bill, called America's Climate Security Act, was presented before a Congressional panel in December 2007. Sponsored by Senators Lieberman and John Warner, the proposed bill put emission limits on the electric utility, transportation, and manufacturing industries, which are the nation's heaviest polluters. That move would cut U.S. greenhouse gas emissions by about 70 percent by 2050, according to the bill's sponsors.

Suing Over Greenhouse Gases

In 2005, more than a dozen states sued the EPA for not doing its job properly. The issue revolved around the levels of carbon dioxide being emitted into the atmosphere by new cars and trucks. The states felt that the EPA's standards were not strict enough and that the agency was allowing the auto industry to raise the amount of toxic emissions its vehicles could legally produce, in defiance of the Clean Air Act.

EPA administrators argued that greenhouse gases such as carbon dioxide weren't covered under the Clean Air Act, and there wasn't enough scientific evidence to prove such emissions caused global warming. On top of that, they denied states the right to make their own regulations regarding vehicle emissions. (In certain situations, the EPA allows local and state governments to create their own regulations, as long as they meet basic agency standards.)

The Circuit Court in Washington, D.C., that originally heard the case in 2005 ruled in favor of the EPA. The case then went before the U.S. Supreme Court, which ruled in April 2007 that greenhouse gases from vehicles are covered under the Clean Air Act, so the EPA could and should regulate these emissions.

The Green Movement

Part political organization, part advocacy group, the Green Movement blends concern for the environment with other social justice issues such as feminism and antidiscrimination. Those involved with the movement want equality and protection, under the law and within government, for all living things and the nature that sustains them.

The Green Movement is grounded in the idea of participatory democracy, which means that everyone within the movement should have a meaningful say in how the government is run. In an attempt to make sure everyone is heard, the Green Movement depends on the frequent exchange of ideas and intense communication among members.

Within the Green Movement are political parties around the world that concentrate on getting movement candidates, called Greens, elected to office at the local, regional, and national levels of government. The platform, or core set of beliefs, of the Green Party in the United States is the very definition of what it means to live green: "Human societies must operate with the understanding

Hundreds of Green Party members have been elected to state and local levels of government in the United States.

that we are part of nature, not separate from nature. We must maintain an ecological balance and live within the ecological and resource limits of our communities and our planet . . . To this end, we must practice agriculture which replenishes the soil; move to an energy efficient economy; and live in ways that respect the integrity of the natural system" (as quoted by the Green Party's Web site).

As of 2008, the Green Party operates in forty-five states and the District of Columbia. Approximately 225 Greens hold office across the country, mostly at the local level. Two Greens have made it to the state level. Greens have been running for president since 1996, when consumer advocate Ralph Nader was the party's candidate.

Nader, who also campaigned for the presidency in 2000 as a Green, made news in 2008 when he refused the Green Party's nomination for president, choosing to run independent of any party.

The Role of Nongovernmental Organizations

Active in politics but not part of the government are what's known as nongovernmental organizations (NGOs). These are nonprofit groups of volunteers who, in an effort to help society as a whole, take action on politically charged issues such as environmentalism.

There are several NGOs that support the same values as people who live green. One of the most well-known NGOs is Greenpeace, founded in Canada in 1971. Best known for its campaigns against whaling and nuclear power, Greenpeace has also tackled global warming and the destruction of the world's ancient forests. The organization made international headlines in 2007 when tests conducted by Greenpeace scientists revealed that electronics manufacturers were polluting the water in underdeveloped nations.

The Natural Resources Defense Council (NRDC) is another NGO that is popular in the living green movement. With a staff of more than three hundred scientists and other specialists, the NRDC lobbies for governmental policies that reduce global warming, halt pollution,

Greenpeace brings the green-living agenda to the attention of people around the world.

and generally protect the environment. The NRDC has taken corporations and the U.S. government to court over violations of the Clean Water and Clean Air acts.

Green Politics at the International Level

Governments have joined forces to help make the lives of people around the world greener. Over the past few decades, a number of international talks and conferences on climate change have occurred, beginning in 1992 with the first United Nations Climate Change Conference. The purpose of these meetings is to come up with a binding agreement among nations that will reduce the progress of global warming. A binding agreement is a contract that obligates the parties who sign it to take action.

Perhaps the most famous example of this is the Kyoto Protocol. Devised in 1997 at the third UN Climate Change Conference, the Kyoto Protocol is an international agreement among many developed nations to reduce greenhouse gas emissions. A promise to reduce green-house gases to 40 percent below 1990 levels, plus a timeframe for steps toward reaching that goal by 2020, are written into the document.

The Kyoto Protocol is covered by global legislation, under the guidance of the United Nations. Each participating nation is responsible for meeting the protocol's requirements, including paying for any technology or equipment necessary to achieve those goals. The agreement is not legally binding until fifty-five countries ratify it, which means they have to formally approve of its methods and try to meet its goals. As of January 2008, thirty-seven developed countries have done so. The United States is not one of those countries.

It is hoped that climate change talks like those in Bangkok, Thailand, will extend the mission of the UN's Kyoto Protocol.

The terms of the Kyoto Protocol end in 2012. It is hoped that other international discussions on climate change, like the U.S.-led conference in Hawaii at the start of 2008 and the next installment of the UN Conference in April of that year, will bring about another agreement to take its place.

Living Green Today

4

Living green has changed quite a bit since the 1960s, when it first became an organized movement in the United States. Back then, living in an environmentally friendly manner was considered an alternative lifestyle, or different from the way most people chose to live. Most Americans were enjoying the benefits that industry and high technology brought to their lives, regardless of what the effect was on the environment. Green was a lifestyle embraced only by hippies—young people who were against the established way of doing things, who distrusted government and its policies, and who often scorned corporate America and its profit-based motives.

That's not the case today. Living green is no longer thought of as alternative. In fact, it is quickly becoming the norm. For example, about thirty-five million Americans make it a point to buy Earth-friendly products, according to a 2006 survey conducted by the global market research firm Mintel International Group. According to a study by the Travel Industry Association of America, more than fifty-five million Americans have shown an interest in sustainable travel, where travelers make it a point to lessen transportation-related carbon emissions and conserve the environment of the place they are visiting.

There are so many areas in which modern society has gone green. The following is a closer look at some environmental trends that have made headlines.

Personal Transportation

As the single largest contributor to human-made greenhouse gases on the planet, cars and trucks are beginning to undergo a green makeover. In the twenty-first century, there have been technological innovations in how these vehicles are built and how they operate. The definition of a green car is one that burns less gas and oil and, subsequently, emits less carbon dioxide and other harmful pollutants. Hybrid and electric cars and trucks have entered the marketplace and have been a big hit with those who have chosen a green lifestyle.

The more popular of the two types with American consumers, the hybrid is a vehicle powered by two sources of energy, typically gas and electricity. Hybrids emit less carbon dioxide than a standard combustion engine vehicle. Simply having two power sources does not make a car green, however. The vehicle must also get better gas mileage and emit less carbon dioxide.

Electric and hybrid vehicles are of great interest to green consumers everywhere.

Sales of hybrid cars soared in 2004 but leveled off somewhat in 2006. Still, a handful of new, small companies started selling hybrid cars in 2007, and well-known manufacturers such as Nissan and Mitsubishi report-edly have environmentally friendly models in the works.

Electric cars run on electricity and are plugged in instead of gassed up when the tank hits empty. The fact that they send no harmful emissions into the atmosphere makes electric cars an extremely green choice in automobiles. One reason electric cars are not more pop-ular, however, is that they have a limited travel range. As reported in the *Washington Post* in 2005, General Motors had manufactured an electric car, called the EV1, in the late 1990s that could be bought in California and Arizona test markets. GM had hoped to offer the EV1 nationwide but wound up scrapping production in 2003 because the cars went only about 140 miles (225 kilometers) before they needed to be recharged. That was inconvenient for motorists, so not enough people bought the cars to make widespread production worthwhile for the company.

As of 2008, electric cars were being made only in small numbers and were not widely available. Automakers are working on new technology that could allow these vehicles to go much farther before needing to be recharged. This, in turn, would increase the electric car's popularity, availability, and profitability, and, therefore, its viability.

Building and Construction

Greening indoors has a positive effect on the great outdoors. The homes in which we live, the offices and buildings in which we work, and the schools in which we study are part of today's green living as well. A green building is one that is built using recycled or eco-friendly materials, uses energy-efficient technology, and maintains healthy indoor air quality.

Several examples of green construction projects have been making headlines. The Freedom Tower and other buildings rising up on New York City's World Trade Center site are using green principles. Several office buildings, including the city halls of Chicago and Atlanta, feature roofs covered in living plants, which provide insulation and reduce water runoff that can damage buildings.

Rooftop gardens save companies energy and money.

According to an article in *USA Today*, builders are going green not only to help the environment, but also because it's a smart business move. New federal buildings must meet green standards, and many individual states require that buildings funded in part or in whole by tax dollars must be green. People trying to live green want homes that match their values. If architects and construction companies want to win these jobs and stay in business, they need to go green themselves.

Driving the green building market in the United States is the Leadership in Energy and Environmental Design (LEED) program of the federal Green Building Council. Gaining LEED certification is important to U.S. builders because it gives their companies official credentials as green businesses. A February 2008 *Syracuse Post-Standard* article stated that approximately 1,300 buildings nationwide already have been certified, and nearly ten thousand more are waiting for their applications to be approved.

Sustainable Eating

An August 2007 *Newsweek* article looked at green living on U.S. college campuses. One of the most prominent measures taken at the featured schools, which included Harvard and Yale universities, was serving locally grown, organic products in their cafeterias and dining halls. As the article pointed out, eating food produced by local farms reduces carbon dioxide emitted when edibles are shipped long distances. The move also keeps small farms in operation, which saves land from being misused or turned over for industrial purposes.

Buying local has been a huge living green trend for years. In 2006, *Time* magazine reported on "locavores," who eat only what is grown or raised no more than 100 miles (161 km) from their homes. The concept has become so popular that "locavore" was named 2007 Word of the Year by the Oxford American Dictionary. The movement toward eating locally not only pops up in news stories but also makes appearances on best-selling book lists across the nation. Author Barbara Kingsolver's *Animal, Vegetable, Miracle* details the year she and her family ate only what they grew themselves or could obtain locally. This and other books with a similar theme, like Michael Pollan's *The Omnivore's Dilemma*, have become big hits, read by millions of people around the world.

Entertainment Spotlight on the Environment

Books aren't the only forms of entertainment that tackle such issues. From movies and television shows with environmental storylines to celebrities promoting an eco-friendly lifestyle, Hollywood has gone totally green. Starting with the documentary *Who Killed the Electric Car?* in 2006, several environmentally themed films have been released. These include the young adult feature *Hoot and the White Planet*, a documentary about wildlife and climate change in Antarctica that has a downloadable online study guide. Similar films are in production.

In addition to sending messages about saving the environment, the Hollywood community has taken action. Many television and movie productions now write scripts on recycled paper and post rewrites electronically. In 2007, *LA Weekly* reported how the television show *24* was going green by using biodiesel generators, low-energy LED lights, and hybrid cars for transportation, among other measures. Also in 2007, iHollywood Forum presented "Hollywood Goes Green," billed as the first trade conference to address environmental issues and green business practices in the entertainment industry.

Celebrities are making good use of their fame to help make the world a greener place. For instance, Leonardo DiCaprio has started a foundation that raises awareness of environmental issues, and he financially

supports the efforts of other groups. The band Pearl Jam donated $100,000 to green organizations in 2006. Singer Sheryl Crow got people's attention when, on her 2007 Stop Global Warming College Tour, she jokingly suggested that people should be restricted to only one square of toilet paper when they visit the restroom. Other newsworthy activities include Cameron Diaz teaming up with former U.S. vice president Al Gore on the Save Our Selves campaign and Brad Pitt working on a green rebuilding of hurricane-devastated New Orleans.

The Greening of American Businesses

Individual efforts to live green go a long way toward sustaining Earth, but industry can have an even larger impact on pollution and greenhouse gas levels. Dedication to living green in America's industrial sector has taken many forms. The National Resources Defense Council reports that many corporations, like Toyota and publishing conglomerate Hearst Corporation, have moved into green buildings constructed especially for them.

Meanwhile, labor unions in the United States are joining forces with environmental groups such as the Sierra Club in order to protect not only the environment but also good-paying jobs and workers' rights. An article in the October 6, 2007, issue of *National Journal* quoted AFL-CIO Industrial Union Council executive director

Robert Baugh as saying, "The one thing that we've managed to do, and that was a breakthrough for the AFL-CIO, was to say that climate change is a problem and we need to do something about it."

Company CEOs are working with environmental groups to pass legislation aimed at reducing greenhouse gases. According to a 2007 posting on CNNMoney.com, corporations such as General Electric and DuPont are part of the United States Climate Action Partnership (USCAP), which seeks to reduce carbon dioxide emissions by up to 80 percent by the year 2050. However, as noted in a March 2008 *Business Week* article, a few of the USCAP member companies also have ties to organizations that oppose stricter regulations, which would force them to spend money so that their factories and offices will meet new federal pollution standards. The world will have to wait and see which side of the environmental debate USCAP companies take in the long run.

The Future of Living Green

5

I n 2007, scientists with the UN's Intergovernmental Panel on Climate Change made the following forecast for the planet through the end of the twenty-first century. The average land temperature should increase by anywhere from 2 to 11 degrees Fahrenheit (roughly 1 to 6 degrees Celsius). Summer heat waves are expected to become more common and unbearable. There will be more rain, and rough weather conditions will likely create more destructive storms than usual. The temperature of the world's oceans will rise, as will sea levels, which would put many island communities and coastal developments underwater.

All of these dire but scientifically rigorous predictions ensure that there will be a profound need for green living in the years to come. Advanced technology, improved sources of energy, and a growing acceptance of environmentalism should guarantee a healthy supply of green options to meet future demand.

Lighting fixtures using energy-saving LED technology are being produced in greater numbers.

Advanced Technology

Advances in technology are making it possible to envision a greener future for the world at large. For instance, electric and hybrid cars have benefited from new battery technology. The development of lithium ion batteries, which are smaller and hold more energy than regular batteries, means these cars can go farther on a single charge.

According to *Popular Mechanics* magazine, researchers at the Massachusetts Institute of Technology (MIT) are working on a project that could replace lithium ion batteries. They have designed a small, lightweight power source called an ultracapacitor that would make engines run smoother and burn less oil, consequently emitting fewer greenhouse gases. Ultracapacitors are made possible because of nanotechnology, which is the design of very small electrical circuits and devices.

Nanotechnology also has made a breakthrough in eco-friendly lighting possible. Light-emitting diodes, or

LEDs, are small, energy-efficient lights used in electronics such as digital clocks. In 2008, scientists in Turkey discovered that covering LEDs in material made up of tiny nanocrystals made them burn brighter and whiter, and they didn't use any more energy than regular LEDs. Researchers believe that this technology could make it possible for energy-saving LEDs to completely replace the incandescent and fluorescent light bulbs used today.

Cleaner Fuels

Researchers continue to develop new ways to power vehicles and machines without nasty consequences, like carbon dioxide emissions and other pollutants. For instance, scientists have created a process that removes almost all of the sulfur in traditional diesel fuel. Sulfur tends to clog up the devices in new car exhaust systems that filter out harmful chemicals such as carbon dioxide. Taking the sulfur out makes car exhaust cleaner.

According to the federal Department of Energy, the United States is also investigating the use of hydrogen fuel cells. This technology involves mixing hydrogen and oxygen to produce electrical power. Instead of toxic exhaust, fuel cells emit only heat and water. So far, the United States has spent about one billion dollars on fuel cell research, and more studies will likely take place in the future.

Another option that has been in the news a lot is biofuels. These are made from renewable resources such as plants. At this point, biofuels are mostly used to power cars. They burn cleaner (without as much toxic exhaust) than fossil fuels such as gasoline and oil. Two main types of biofuel are used in the world today— biodiesel and ethanol. Biodiesel is made from soybeans, while ethanol comes from corn or sugarcane. Oil from these plants is either mixed with various chemicals to make biodiesel or fermented to make ethanol. Fermentation is when the sugars and carbohydrates in plants are combined with yeast to produce alcohol.

Countries in the European Union already use biofuels on a regular basis. Biodiesel and ethanol have slowly made their way into the American market as well. As part of its 2007 energy bill, the U.S. Congress declared that the country should increase production of ethanol as an alternative fuel for automobiles.

Not just cars can benefit from biofuels. As reported in several newspapers, including the *Wall Street Journal* and the *New York Times*, a Virgin Airlines flight flew from London, England, to Amsterdam, the Netherlands, in February 2008 using a mixture of about 80 percent regular jet kerosene and 20 percent biofuel made from nut and coconut oil.

Biofuels Controversy

Even though they are a greener alternative to gas and oil, biofuels are not a perfect energy source. First, the energy used to grow, harvest, and ferment the crops that create these fuels contributes to the buildup of greenhouse gases. Then there is the issue of land use. Some people are afraid that because there is a lot of money to be made growing

Biofuels, which are popular at many European service stations, are not without their problems.

crops to make biofuels, farmers will use most or all of their land for this purpose only. The result would be less land on which to grow crops for humans to eat, so there would be a shortage of certain items in the supermarket. The shortage could drive up the price of food.

Another land-use concern is that forests and wilderness areas will be turned into farmland in order to keep up with the high demand for biofuels. That means cutting down trees and tearing up other plants that filter carbon dioxide out of the air. Loss of these natural areas to farming would mean higher levels of carbon dioxide in the atmosphere and accelerated climate change.

Scientists have started looking for alternative biofuel sources that don't misuse natural resources and can be collected without producing extra greenhouse gas emissions. Algae and fibers from natural plant, tree, and agricultural waste (dead leaves, grass clippings, etc.) are two sources that show promise and may be investigated further.

Fresh Alternatives

In addition to new energy sources, researchers are concentrating on extra ways to use green energy sources that already exist. For instance, solar energy technology has been a popular alternative energy source since the 1970s. But now the panels that collect the sun's rays and generate electricity are being applied to everything from kitchen appliances and cars to, in the near future, laptop computers and handheld electronics chargers. As featured in a November 2007 issue of *Popular Mechanics*, there's even the *Solar Impulse*, a small solar-powered airplane.

The business section of the March 6, 2008, *New York Times* carried a story about a growing trend among utility companies to build solar power plants. Hundreds of solar panels are placed in the desert, where they convert the sun's energy into steam that moves a turbine—a metal cylinder with blades that catch the rising vapor. The moving turbine generates electricity. Utility companies that provide electricity in the American West, including

California and Arizona, have committed to the building of several solar power plants. Experts expect plans for additional plants will be made in the near future.

New Attitudes

As increasing amounts of scientific evidence show that human activity contributes to global warming, attitudes about green living are changing. More and more people are beginning to realize the personal, local, and global benefits of living in a way that saves natural resources.

Our governmental, business, religious, and cultural leaders offer guidance. Politicians such as former vice president Al Gore and several U.S. congressional representatives hold hearings and write legislation dealing with environmental issues. Corporate CEOs join forces with environmental advocacy groups, while the pope (the head of the Catholic Church) declares that "ecological offenses" are a sin. Celebrities influence our increasingly positive attitudes toward green living by setting an example of how to live in greater harmony with nature.

Americans have varying levels of interest in the green movement. However, as time goes by and more scientific evidence comes to light, living green will probably become the "new normal" in the twenty-first century, the way most of us happily live our lives.

Myths and Facts

Myth: "Going Green" is a radical response to a problem—global warming—that most people are not even convinced is real.

Fact: Eighty-three percent of Americans now believe that global warming is a "serious problem." Thousands of Web sites, organizations, magazines, and books are devoted to the promotion of green lifestyles. Major corporations now produce green products and adopt ecologically friendly practices. Locally produced produce and products are available nationwide.

Myth: Going green is expensive.

Fact: Locally grown produce and other products cost less than goods shipped from hundreds or thousands of miles away. Home-grown produce saves even more money. Cutting back on energy consumption will result in lower utility bills. Using a bike instead of a car will eliminate gas bills, repair costs, and insurance premiums. Many states and localities offer tax or other financial incentives for going green.

Myth: Global warming and climate change is so huge that one individual's actions will have no positive effect.

Fact: Making a few simple and painless changes to your lifestyle can result in a drastically smaller individual carbon footprint. Individuals can reduce their carbon footprint by hundreds of thousands, if not millions, of pounds of carbon dioxide over the course of their lives.

Glossary

amendment A changed or added improvement.

carbon dioxide An important greenhouse gas, produced in mass quantity by the burning of fossil fuels.

consensus A general agreement among many people.

incandescent Giving off visible light; incandescent light bulbs are used by most people, but they are no longer the most energy-efficient light bulb. Compact florescent light bulbs (CFLs) are far more energy efficient and long-lasting.

innovation Something new and unique; an improvement upon an earlier model.

locavore A person who eats only food grown locally, usually no more than 100 miles (161 km) from his or her home.

nanotechnology The design of very small, even microscopic electrical circuits and devices.

pollinate To fertilize.

stewardship Taking care of and looking out for the best interests of something, often a piece of land or territory.

turbine A metal cylinder with blades that catch rising steam vapor to generate electricity.

ultracapacitor A greener energy source that could replace the batteries in electric and hybrid cars.

For More Information

Earthwatch Institute
3 Clock Tower Place, Suite 100
Box 75
Maynard, MA 01754
(800) 776-0188
Web site: http://www.earthwatch.org
Earthwatch Institute is an international nonprofit organization that gives people the opportunity to join scientific research teams around the world. This firsthand experience promotes the understanding and action necessary to achieve a sustainable environment.

Environment Canada
70 Crémazie Street
Gatineau, QC K1A 0H3
Canada
(819) 997-2800
(800) 668-6767 (toll free in Canada only)
Web site: http://www.ec.gc.ca
Environment Canada works to preserve and enhance the quality of the natural environment in Canada. It also conserves the country's natural resources and coordinates environmental policies and programs for the federal government.

Global Green USA

2218 Main Street, 2nd Floor

Santa Monica, CA 90405

(310) 581-2700

Web site: http://www.globalgreen.org

A national arm of the international environmental organization Green Cross, Global Green USA merges innovative research, community-based projects, and advocacy to solve pressing environmental challenges. The goal is to reconnect humans with nature.

Web Sites

Due to the changing nature of Internet links, Rosen Publishing has developed an online list of Web sites related to the subject of this book. This site is updated regularly. Please use this link to access this list:

http://www.rosenlinks.com/itn/ligr

For Further Reading

Clemens Warrick, Karen. *John Muir: Crusader for the Wilderness.* Berkeley Heights, NJ: Enslow Publishers, 2002.

Davis, Brangien, and Katharine Wroth. *Wake Up and Smell the Planet: The Non-Pompous, Non-Preachy Grist Guide to Greening Your Day.* Seattle, WA: Mountaineers Books, 2007.

Morris, Stephen. *New Village Green: Living Light, Living Local, Living Large.* Gabriola Island, BC, Canada: New Society Publishers, 2007.

Rogers, Elizabeth, and Thomas M. Kostigen. *The Green Book.* New York, NY: Three Rivers Press, 2007.

Sivertsen, Linda, and Tosh Sivertsen. *Generation Green: The Ultimate Teen Guide to Living an Eco-Friendly Life.* New York, NY: Simon Pulse, 2008.

Bibliography

Brown Weiss, Edith, ed. *Environmental Change and International Law: New Challenges and Dimensions.* Tokyo, Japan: United Nations University Press, 1992.

Burros, Marian. "Preserving Fossil Fuels and Nearby Farmland by Eating Locally." *New York Times*, April 25, 2007, p. F10.

Elgin, Ben. "Green—Up to a Point." *Business Week*, Issue 4073, March 3, 2008, pp. O25–26.

Gari, Lutfallah. "Arabic Treatises on Environmental Pollution Up to the End of the Thirteenth Century." *Environment and History*. Isle of Harris, England: White Horse Press, 2002.

Green Party of the United States. "About Us." Retrieved February 2008 (http://www.gp.org/about.shtml).

Grove, Richard. "Climatic Fears: Colonialism and the History of Environmentalism." *Harvard International Review*, Vol. 23, Issue 4, Winter 2002, pp. 50–56.

Herring, David. "Earth's Temperature Tracker." Goddard Institute of Space Studies. November 2007. Retrieved February 2008 (http://www.giss.nasa.gov/research/features/temptracker/).

Jewett, Thomas. "Thomas Jefferson: Agronomist." Archiving Early America. 2005. Retrieved February

2008 (http://www.earlyamerica.com/review/2005_
summer_fall/agronomist.htm).

McCartney, Scott. "Virgin Puts Biofuels on Maiden
Voyage." *Wall Street Journal*, Vol. 251, Issue 46,
February 26, 2008, pp. D1–D4.

Natural Resources Defense Council. "The Story of Silent
Spring." April 1997. Retrieved February 2008 (http://
www.nrdc.org/health/pesticides/hcarson.asp).

Oreskes, Naomi. "Beyond the Ivory Tower: The Scientific
Consensus on Climate Change." *Science*, December 3,
2004. Retrieved February 2008 (http://www.
sciencemag.org/cgi/content/full/306/5702/1686).

Ritter, John. "Buildings Designed in Cool Shades of
'Green.'" *USA Today*, March 2004. Retrieved March
2008 (http://www.usatoday.com/news/nation/
2004-03-30-sustainable-usat_x.htm).

Roosevelt, Margot. "The Lure of the 100-Mile Diet."
Time, Vol. 167, Issue 24, June 12, 2006, p. 78.

Roosevelt, Theodore. *Theodore Roosevelt: An
Autobiography*. Revised edition. New York, NY:
Charles Scribner and Sons, 2006.

Schneider, Greg, and Kimberly Edds. "Fans of GM
Electric Car Fight the Crusher." *Washington Post*,
March 10, 2005, p. A01.

Scott, Alex. "Leading Electronics Makers Tagged for
Polluting the Environment." *Chemical Week*, Vol. 169,
Issue 9, March 14, 2007, p. 15.

Sofge, Erik. "MIT Builds Efficient Nanowire Storage to Replace Car Batteries." *Popular Mechanics*, February 2008. Retrieved March 2008 (http://www.popularmechanics.com/science/research/4252623.html?series=19).

Streater, Scott. "Living Green and Meaning It." McClatchy Newspapers. October 2007. Retrieved February 2008 (http://www.azcentral.com/news/green/articles/1002livinggreen.html).

U.S. Department of Energy. "Hydrogen Fuel Cells." DOE Hydrogen, Fuel Cells and Infrastructure Technologies Program Fact Sheet. Retrieved March 2008 (http://www1.eere.energy.gov/hydrogenandfuelcells/pdfs/doe_h2_fuelcell_factsheet.pdf).

Van Schagen, Sarah. "15 Green Musicians and Bands." *Grist*, June 2007. Retrieved March 2008 (http://www.grist.org/news/maindish/2007/06/22/musicians).

Vertovec, Steven, and Darrell Addison Posey. *Globalization, Globalism, Environment, and Environmentalism: Consciousness of Connections.* New York, NY: Oxford University Press, 2003.

Wald, Matthew L. "Turning Glare into Watts." *New York Times*, March 6, 2008, p. C1.

Weart, Spencer. "The Discovery of Global Warming." American Institute of Physics. June 2007. Retrieved February 2008 (http://www.aip.org/history/exhibits/climate).

Index

About the Author

Jeanne Nagle is a writer and editor who has a great interest in environmental issues. She is the author of several other books and articles on living green, including *Smart Shopping: Shopping Green* and *Reducing Your Carbon Footprint at School*, written for Rosen Publishing.

Photo Credits

Cover (top left and top right), pp. 8, 30, 38, 40, 42, 47, 51 © Getty Images; cover (bottom), pp. 4, 5, 10, 15, 26, 28, 36, 37 © AFP/Getty Images; p. 6 © Jeff Greenberg/The Image Works; p. 12 © Newscom.com; pp. 16, 20 Library of Congress Prints and Photographs Division; p. 18 © AP Photos; p. 23 National Library of Medicine; p. 24 © Time-Life Pictures/Getty Images; p. 27 © Paramount Classics/Everett Collection; p. 48 © AP Photos.

Designer: Tom Forget; Photo Researcher: Marty Levick